Mother, (v)

Anne Marie Wells

Cinnamon Press
:: small miracles from distinctive voices ::

Published by Cinnamon Press
www.cinnamonpress.com

ISBN 978-1-78864-151-7

British Library Cataloguing in Publication Data. A CIP record for this book can be obtained from the British Library.

Designed and typeset in Bodoni by Cinnamon Press. Cover design by Adam Craig.

Cinnamon Press is represented by Inpress Ltd.

Acknowledgements

Some of the poems have been previously published in the following: 'A Fig Tree of My Own', *Beyond the Veil Press*, 2022; 'Cherimoya', *Reflections Anthology*, Maryland Writers Association, 2023; '[Dumbo broke my heart as a child]', 'Miscarriage I', 'Miscarriage II', 'Mother, (v)' and 'One for the Forest', *SixFold*, 2023.

About the Author

Anne Marie Wells (She | They) is the author of *Survived By: A Memoir in Verse + Other Poems* (Curious Corvid Publishing, 2023), the inaugural winner of the Wanderlust Travel Book Award for her memoir, *Happy Iceland*, through Wild Dog Press (pending publication), and the 2023 winner of the Cinnamon Press Chapbook Contest for her collection, *Mother, (v)*. She won the 2023 Maryland Writers Association Poetry Contest, the 2023 Jackson Hole Poetry Box Contest, 2023 DC Public Library Haiku Contest, was long-listed for the International Erbacce Prize in Poetry, and was short-listed for the inaugural Emma Howell Rising Poet Award. She was the winner of the 2021 Crow House Press Poetry Competition, earned the 2021 Peter K. Hixson Memorial award in poetry presented by Writer's Relief, and was a 2021 Wyoming Woman of Influence nominee in the arts category for amplifying the voices of the LGBTQ and disabled communities through her writing. She received the 2020 Milestone Award presented by Wyoming Writers, Inc., and the 2020 Rising Star Award presented by the Jackson Hole Chamber of Commerce. She is the lead faculty for the DC Chapter of the Community Literature Initiative poetry publishing program through the Sims Library of Poetry and strategic partnership fellow for The Poetry Lab.

Contents

Mother, (v)

Mother, (n)

my belly   still
empty   hungry for
my waist my breasts my
heart to ripen into a mother
rewind through   years
of   missed connections
the time i'd said   i wouldn't
settle   when i thought i had
all the time to wait   now
regret   bleeds through lace
lingerie   so quiet   so still
so flat   my belly

Who knows why
some oak leaves remain

latched to the branches
that sprouted them, enduring the lion

gales of January, the grizzly hale

of March, while others float
effortlessly to the ground,

never meant to hold on.

Miscarriage I

Matryoshka

[   ] shriveled
and so did I, this second
iteration of myself,
this version that existed
between knowledge
and disappearance.

Where does the veil go?
The one I did not know
I wore until it became
a shroud, leaving
me a smaller shell
of who I once was.

Devoured

He told me to remember when we were only
sculpted shadows of a candle choir, when we forced
our focus away from our buttons and belts and onto
each other's faces. When it was much too late, but
we wouldn't say so, only breathed in and out our
meaningless blatherings like a flute playing no
melody in particular but still ringing pleasant to
the ear. We are still those people, even in this
basement apartment with no air. We fill the gaps
with new questions, new answers, like feeding
pages from the PennySaver to a one-log fire,
keeping the night lit between us in staccato

bolts. The hours sway, despite our best efforts, in
their lazy hammocks into tomorrow, further away
from the child we would have loved. Our pupils
widen at any spark of goodbye that whistles out
from our fire; we blow them to ash before they can
land. I'm pretty sure there was a meteor shower
that night. I wasn't looking, but my ribs felt a city
full of people making wishes at the same time. I
tallied the specks of moon dust as they buried us
in an hourglass lying forehead to forehead
breathing each other's breath, his hand motionless
at the hem of my dress, my hand gripped onto a
star-blazing hope from the back of his neck.

Perimenopause

A ribcage
After Athena Liu

it's probably too late for me now at forty,
[she]
chants to herself as she swipes through the leftovers;
[prays]
her uterine lining remains hospitable
[like]
it was twenty years earlier when she was just
[a]
weak-heart finding self-value in male attention,
[worn]
like a bull-horn buckle on a dimestore belt, hum
[drum]
until she slunk like an ermine through protesters
[for]
mifepristone and misoprostol. white-lipped. no
[hands]
to cup her face, no tongue to say, You're not a slut,
[to]
whistle ABBA tunes in the car on the way home.
[still]
never had a romance that passed the second year.
[touch]
after touch—if it was love—none ever grew on
[her.]

A ribcage is a poetic form invented by poet Athena Liu consisting of 12 alternating, 12-syllable lines and a monosyllabic word in brackets. At the end of the text, the bracketed words — or spine — are read from top to bottom.

Cherimoya

I have no business trying to grow cherimoyas
in the outskirts of D.C.   but there she is

      a foot tall   leaves like a child
's drawing of leaves   bobbing about a cardboard box
in the back of my Subaru   a placeholder

        I make a place for her in the living room
—where all the living is supposed to happen—

center stage on the coffee table
direct sun   under the heating vent

        to trick her into thinking she's back in the Andes
instead of a basement apartment.

              When might she swell
into a protective fruit in hopes
her seeds will find a life of their own in this world?

        Maybe I'll be eighty when I wrest an emerald
babe from her twiggy arms   each of my pruned fingers flush
with a leathery heart of skin

          won't even bother to wash the thing—I'll know
where it's been—   no plate   no towel

        I'll cleave open its flesh   dig out its center with a spike
-tipped spoon   *I used to eat these every morning*
when I lived in Coimbra   I'll say to no one   spitting
out a seed like a black checker

Back when I was young   never thinking
about the time dripping from my nails
*   or the pool of years left behind on the sticky counter*

Late

I whisper out loud and in silence through my mind the way I used to
speak to the ghosts I wasn't sure lived in my childhood basement.

Hi. It's just me.
I feel you there. I think. I hope.
  I hope you feel happy here. I feel
        happy you're here. I hope I'm not
              making you up. Show me
                a sign if I'm not making you up.
                   Don't be afraid. I'm not

                   afraid of you.

                 I hope you stay.

                 If you'd like to,

                 I'd love to meet you

                 sometime soon.

Beacon

My daydreaming turns toward the lighthouse keeper, step after step spiraling up the stone tower,   December's frigid   nights   still clinched deep within its atoms. The turret glass cleared, wicks trimmed, an invisible voice through the fire's steady   pulse   shouts over   the   fathoms: *Here,   here,   here   is home, home, home.*

[Dumbo broke my heart as a child]

Dumbo broke my heart as a child, and still I cannot watch, cannot even think about that movie. My ribs disintegrate on themselves, my mother's name appears in their dust each time Mrs. Jumbo reaches her trunk through the jail car bars to rock her wing-eared baby while all the other babies sleep spooned in their cages. Five, seven, fourteen, thirty-six. I never grew out of it. The violins introduce 'Baby Mine' before the choir joins in. Mrs. Jumbo's trunk strokes her baby's face in recognition. Tears form in Dumbo's eyes, then my own. I'd break through my mother's door, words no longer words. Spit and sound. Ululations. A cicada's percussion across her lap, pleading for her to soothe my rattles, lull me back from the cruel-hearted circus, make me forget the cartoon calf walking away, waving goodbye to his mother with his trunk. *Dumbo again? You know you can't handle that movie, she'd groan. Don't watch it anymore.* Her arms wouldn't always be there to swaddle my spiracles. She tried to teach me, but I'm still learning: With all the suffering in this world, all the agony I would endure in this life, why cause myself more? And on purpose?

Not Pregnant

The stick sits on the sink staring
back at me, stoic as a still life.

I return an hour after my forfeit, looking
for a rematch. At night, mouthwash

burns my gums as I glance at the trash,
glance again, glance a third time, bend

over for a closer look. At the end
of the week, I rustle through cotton

swabs, used tissues, floss just to look
one more time, just to hear it yell No

one more time, in case it had changed
its mind, in case I misheard its response

each of the fourteen times before.

The fox lay mangled

on the side of the highway, dead, of course, in a pool of ended potential. The days she once knew—free but bound to her role in predator and prey, shackled to the means by which she survived—were over, and her shredded pelt could not, at this point, even find use in a furrier's workshop had she surrendered her dignity in exchange for a vain existence traveling on the hood of a coat in the upper echelons of the city, feeling the arias of sopranos resonate in the tips of her fur from a Kennedy Center box seat or the September whir of the turnpike whooshing through her cayenne and ginger tones from the passenger side of a top-down Aston Martin.

The beast would never know what tragedies would have hit her if the tires had not, and yet, she still had work to do in this world. She was no longer just a fox, but had she ever really been? If she lived on now within the veins of vultures and crows, raccoons and coyotes, within the grass peeking out from the gravel, hadn't she, too, always lived as a composite of the past? An amalgam of all the realities that were once possible—the ones that still are and the ones that are no longer. One life had come and gone, sure. But what is it to release one unrealized dream when standing at the threshold of and gone, sure. But what is it to release one unrealized dream when standing at the threshold of

infinite what ifs?

[   ] Sentence

or if i'm still being punished

for when i was once
a twenty-year-old, fuck-up

of a kid, just wanting to move
out west or to study in europe,

just wanting to be wanted, wanting
to live my life in a world where my

biology didn't determine
my choices, haven't i served

my penance? haven't i prayed enough
hail mary's to be forgiven for saying

no to motherhood half my life ago?
oh, my god, my god, blessed mother:

i am ready now. i am ready now.

One for the Forest

The clouds paint the sky in watercolors
          as I commit my feet to the earth blessing
the worms and voles   blessing the needle
-laden soil weaving between my toes as I sink
          beneath the surface   Thrushes play their tinny flutes
and I laugh at the quilt of doubt I patched
          from years of revolving doors
and fire escapes Why has it felt so hard to find freedom
in stillness?   The way trees have done for ages?
          Instead of asking if I can endure the months
heavy   with bitter snow falls   with the trust
needed to swear   nothing will change   if
I will tire of this view after   I let my skin harden
          let my hair fill with the smell of dust   can I
intertwine my branches and vow to bloom a ring
for each year I've forgiven myself?   Can I keep pushing toward
          a new unknown something?   Can I settle
then   into an evergreen
          existence?   Everything else kaleidoscoping around
                              just me?

A Fig Tree of My Own

As it has gone, it still goes:
while one foot stays in the present,

the other wriggles free to worlds
I have yet to visit, The Unknown,

hypotheticals I've yet to pick apart,
a universe of potential, slippery

in the depths of dreams and being.
It *me faz um cafuné*, lures me

with ephemera. The sun slices through
green and silver canopies, dares me to

say yes to each of my possible lives.

my eyes are not eyes   lights illume when
the cranks jig the curtains up   my hands
are not hands   mechanics   clutch   the
controls operate an illusion on a rotary of cogs
        my skin is not skin   only a sheath acting
as scaffolding acting as a barrier in motion linked
to gears and fine fibers to sense cold and moments
of awe   My bones are not bones
              rods and piping   bolts and
brackets wrought and hammered mounted to
swivels and pulley systems   my lungs are not
lungs just steam engine bellows programmed to
expand and contract   no
questions just algorithms and mathematics
but my heart is still a heart   a muscle
a glitch   tugging to the left as if in
protest to the metal and rust
still feeling the disappointments of the past despite
the grease   no pillows or blankets
no art on the walls   no candles or novelty
towels   steel and wire   a reminder i
once wanted to be more than machinery
the passerines sing their arias in the yard next door
but their songs don't linger in the corners of the
halls   the breeze of their wings does not sweep
eddies of wayward petals from the neighbor's
marigolds over the threshold
i don't leave seeds in the feeder for them
to fly off with in their beaks   they stopped
visiting   stopped looking for reasons to visit
                              long ago

Miscarriage II

Mother, (v)

no handprints on mirrors no play-doh
crusted into carpet   no penciled scribbles
on the wall to mark each year of   growth
i sleep   through the night   only wake
for the bathroom   no tiny voice cries for me
to save them   from a nightmare   i peek through
the door to the other room   it's empty
except for boxes of winter clothes and photo albums   i leave
my lipsticks and perfume   strewn around the sink
with my bobby pins   no pint-sized toothbrush leans against mine
no toys in primary colors line the tub's edge   no shampoo
for sensitive eyes   i've never sighed over wet towels in a heap
on the bathroom floor   or vacuumed crumbs out of the creases
of a carseat   never folded laundry that wasn't my own   never
bleached a karate gi   never listened to a hissing violin with a smile
no mickey mouse bandages in the first-aid kit   my lips
have never touched a bruise   i leave candles lit on the nightstand   eat
popcorn for dinner in front of the tv   the table in the kitchen has only one
chair   i don't remind anyone   to chew with mouth closed
or that breakfast is the most important meal of the day   maybe i'll fly
to portugal just because   dance to fado   or shop
for ceramic whatever and cork such-and-such   no one needs me
to pack their   tuna fish and potato chip sandwich   before school
or to kiss them goodbye   before they run   to the bus
no one asks if i can read   *The Monster at the End of This Book*
four times before they fall asleep   no one weeps
in my absence   i go by no other name
i worry over no one   no one worries over me